Mmmmm!

by Lada Josefa Kratky

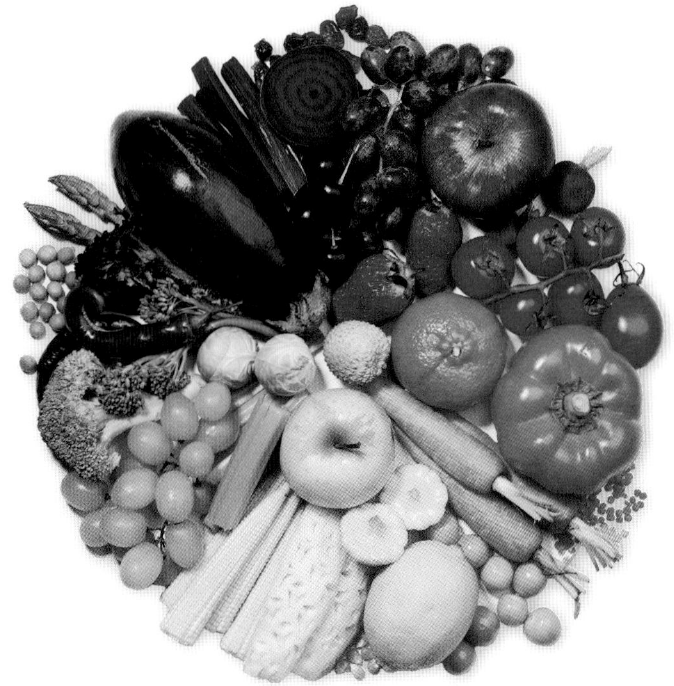

NATIONAL GEOGRAPHIC
School Publishing

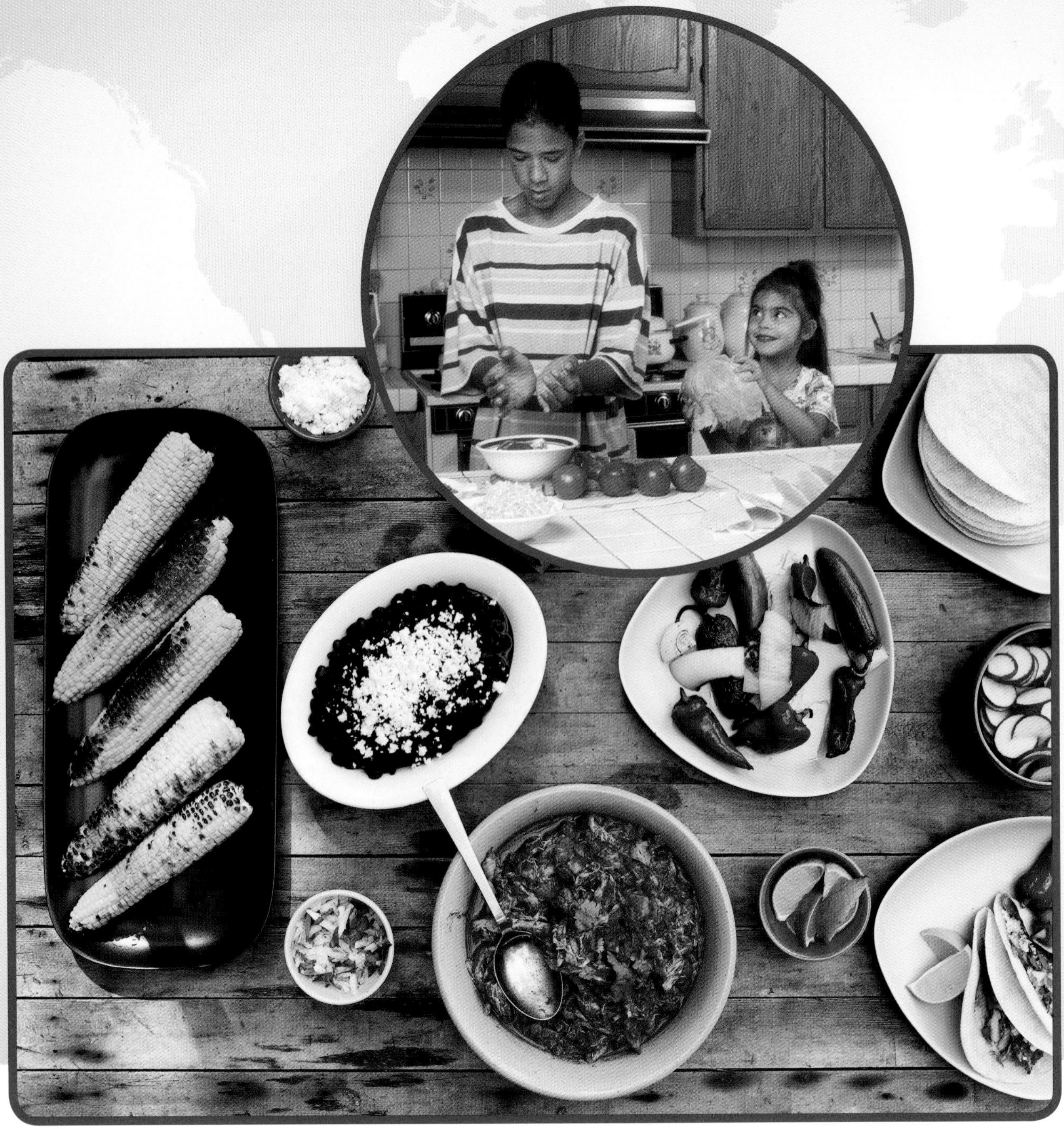

Mmmmmmm!

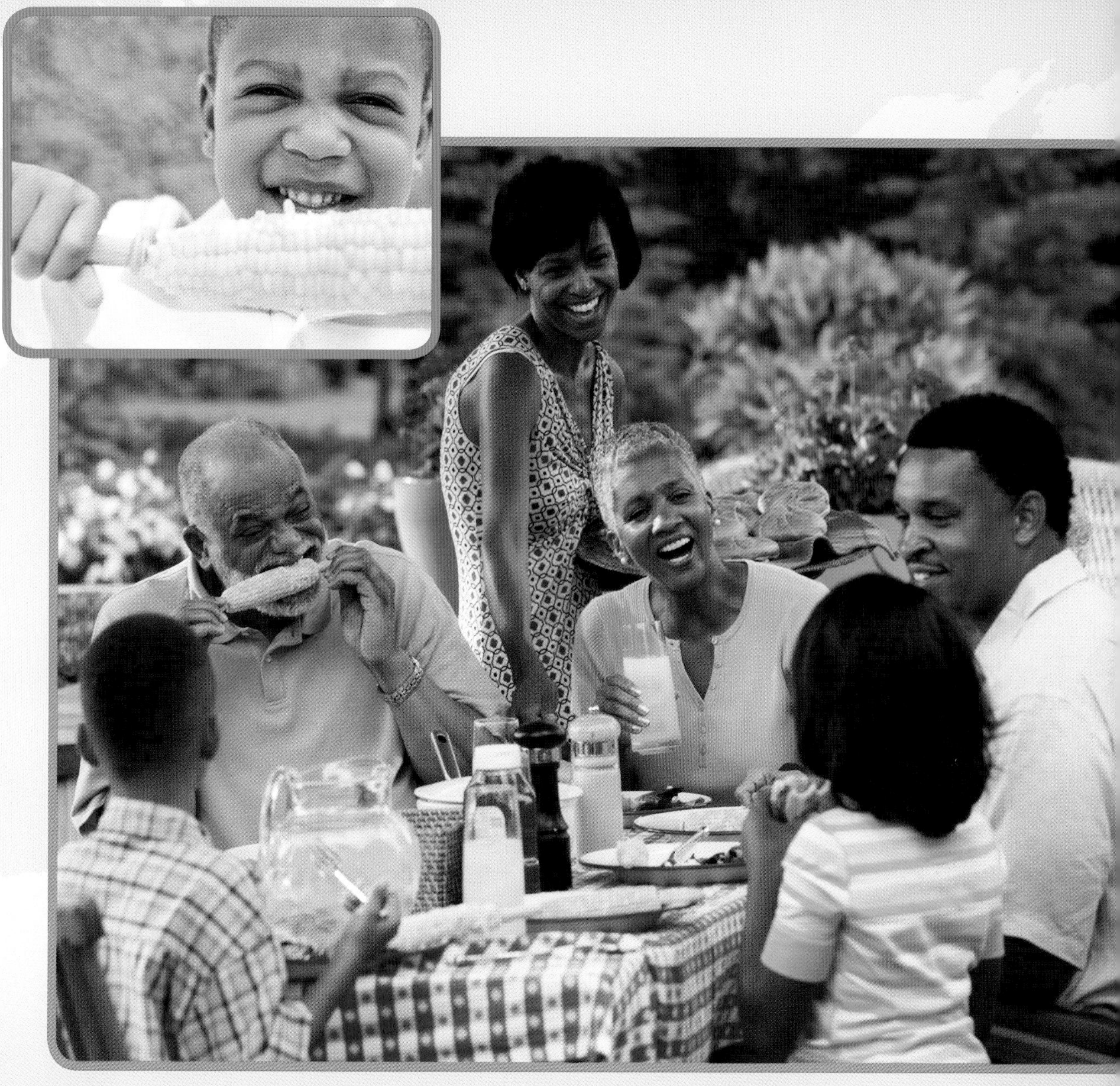

Mmmmmmm!

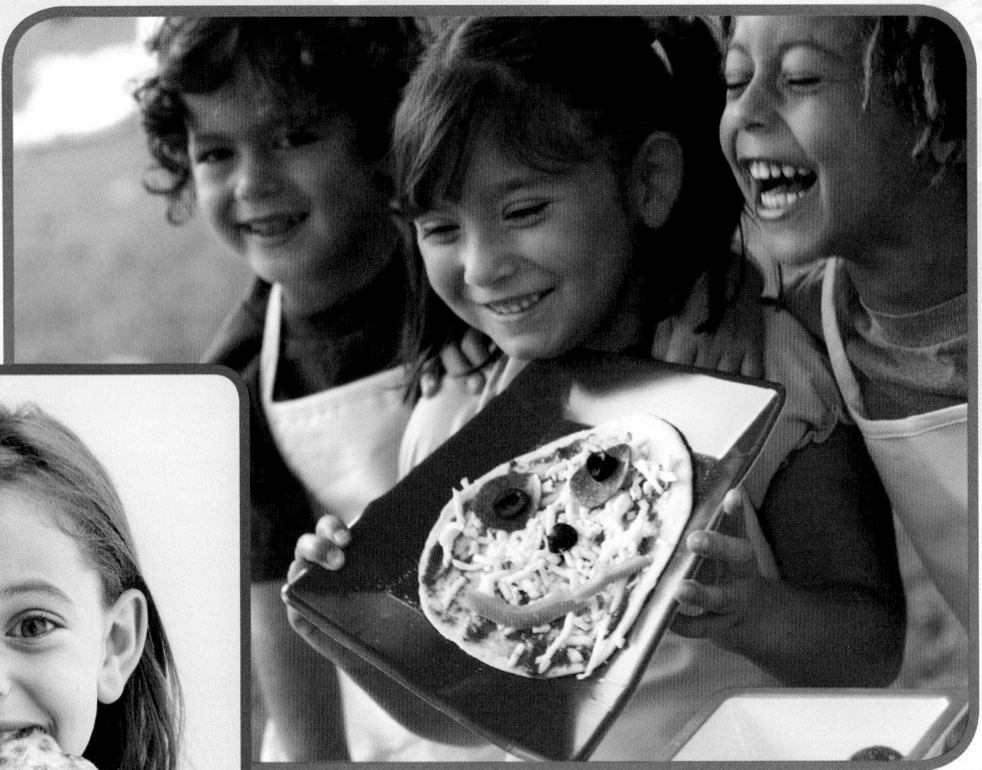

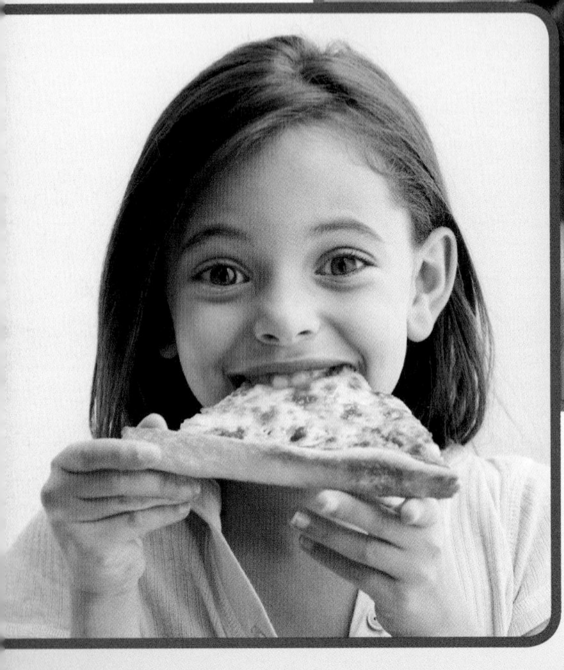

Mmmmmm!

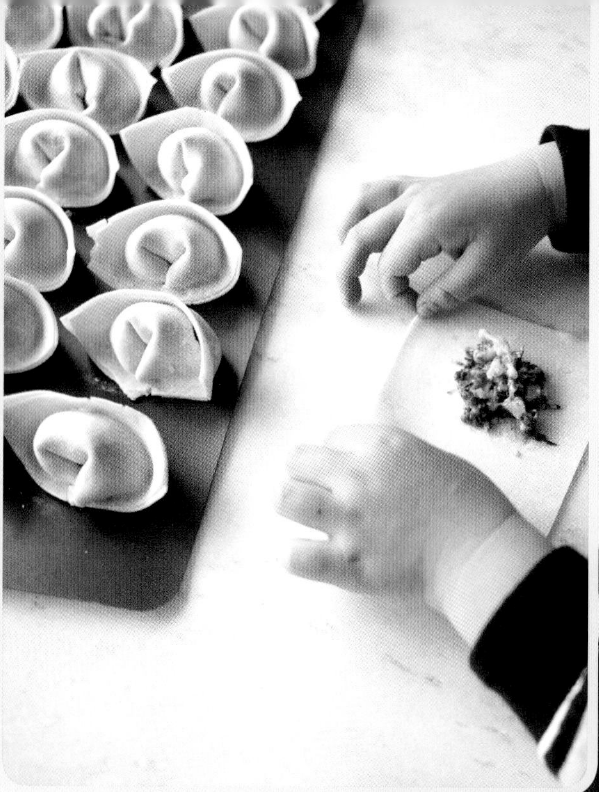

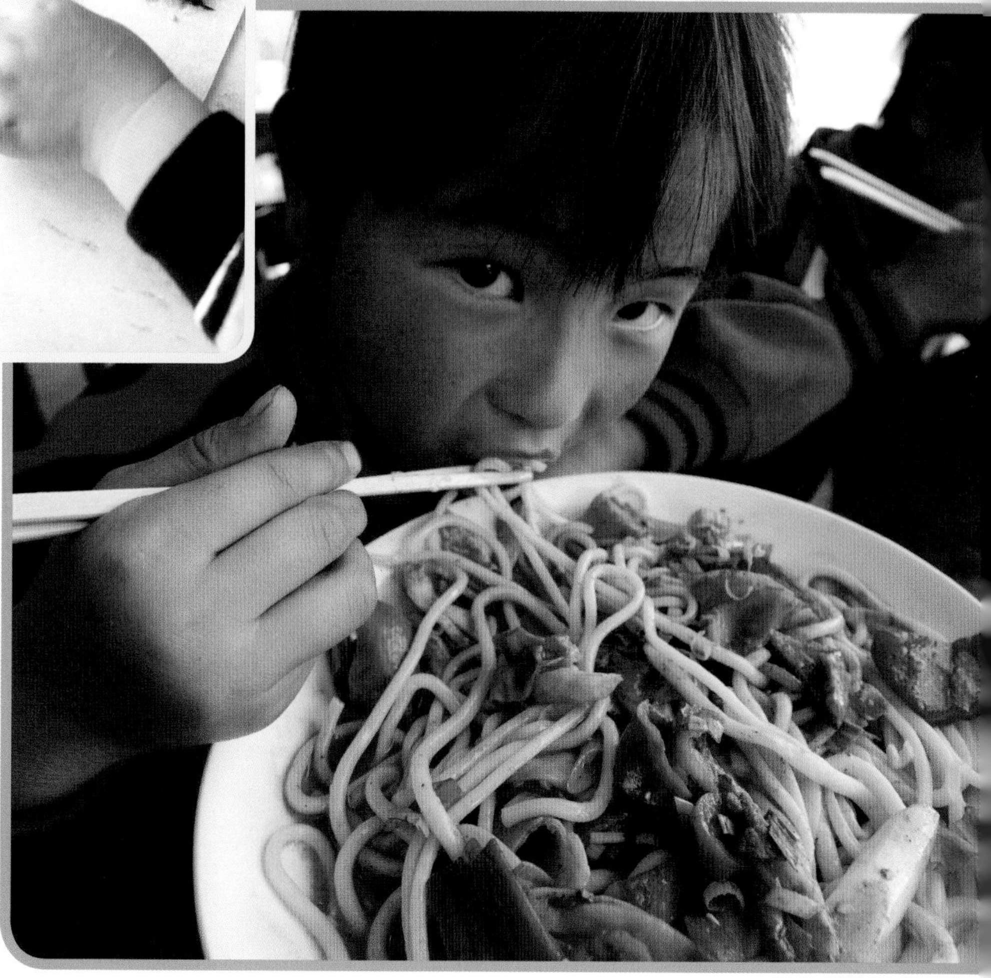

Mmmmmmm!

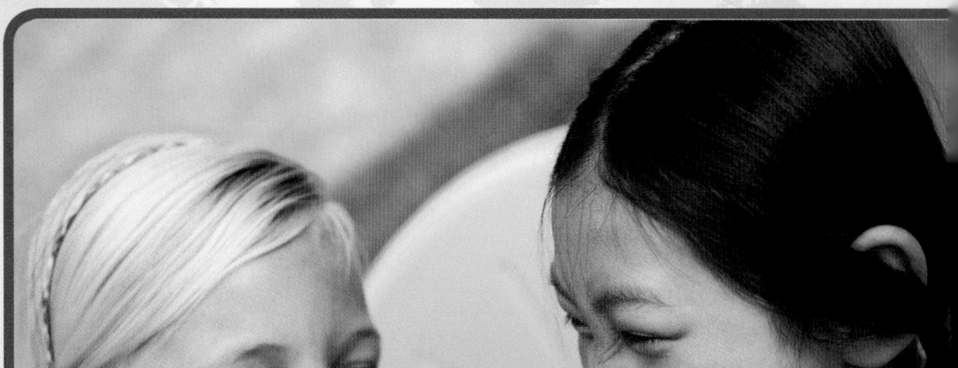

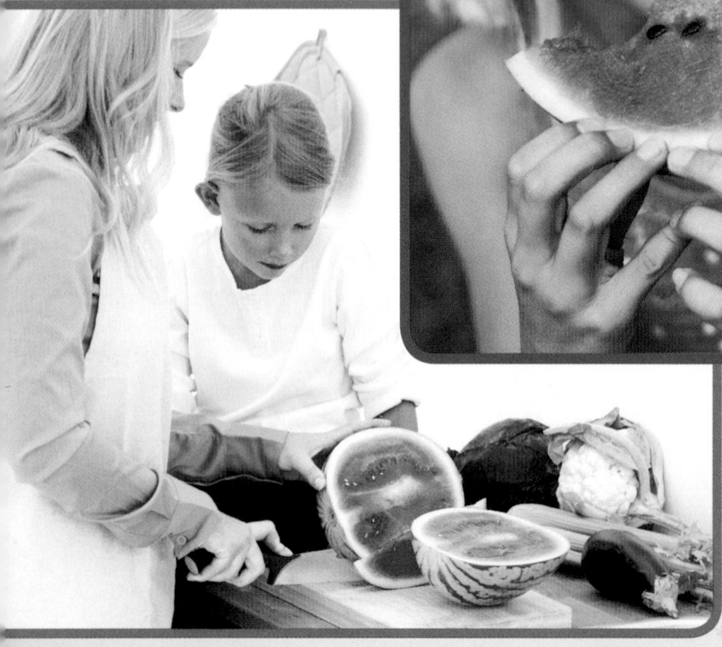

Mmmmmmm!

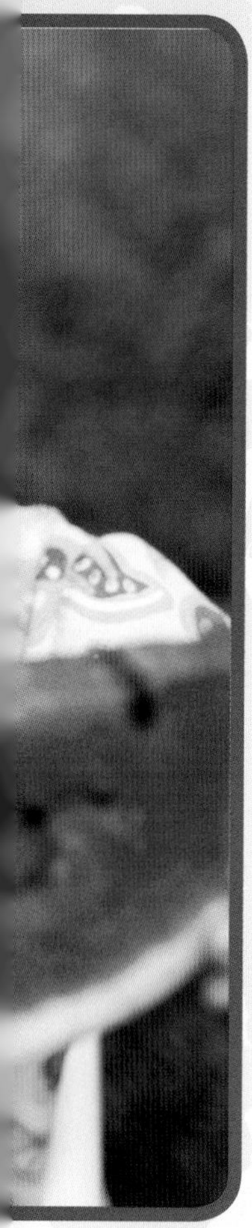

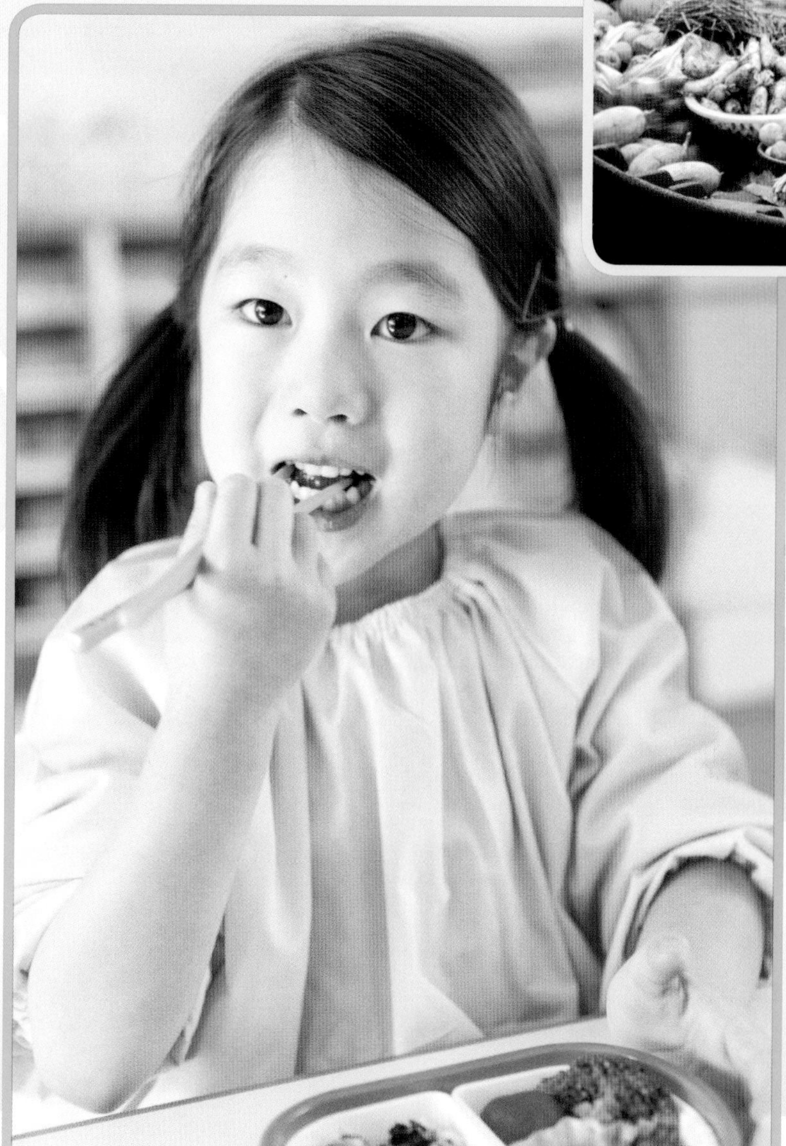

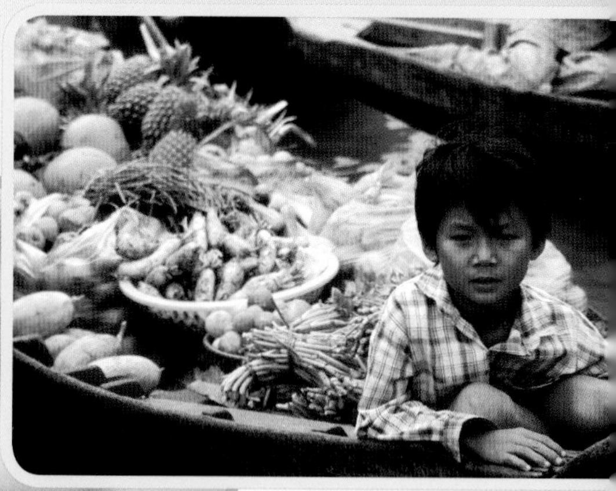

Mmmmmmm!

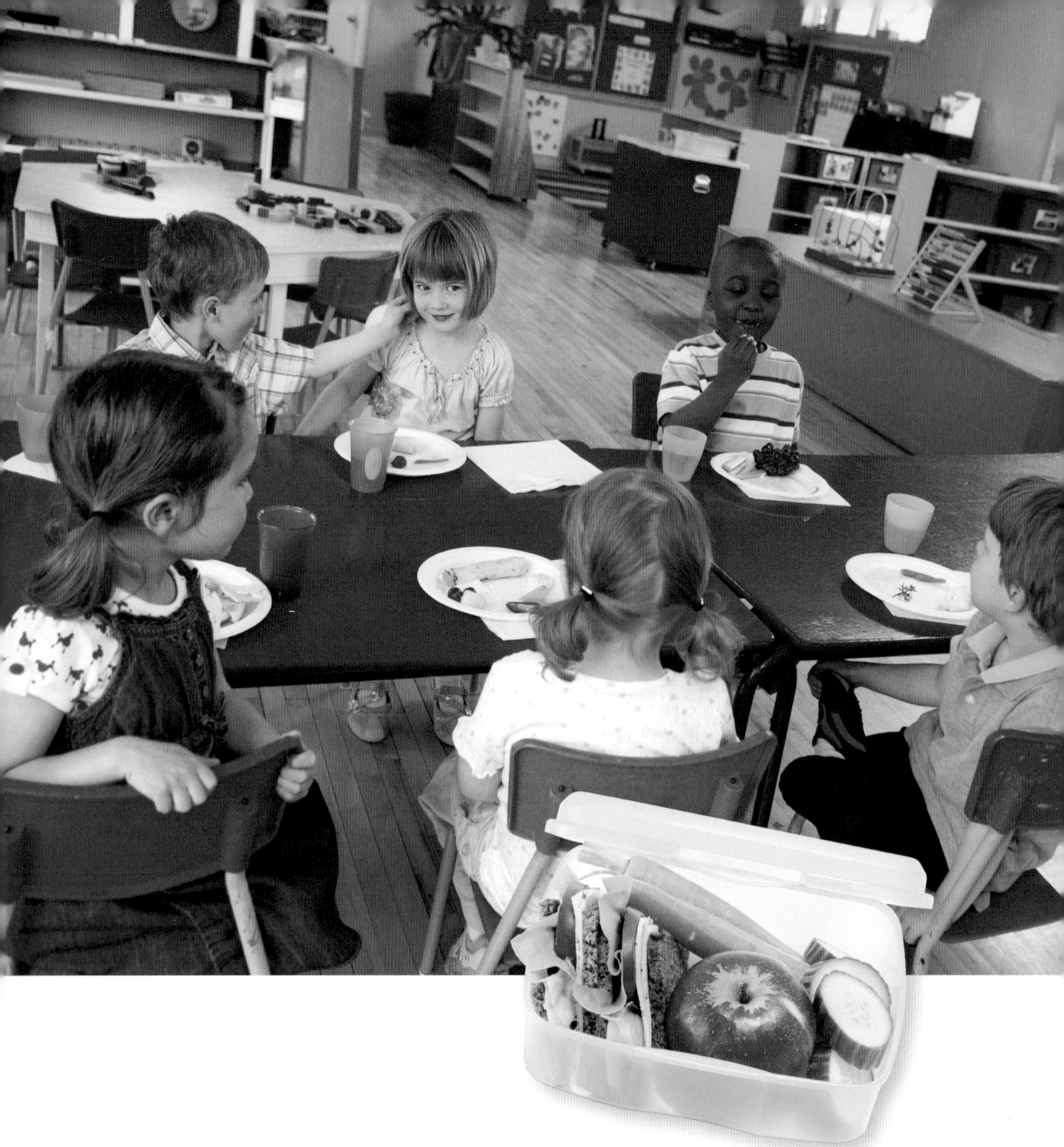

Mmmmmm!